POETRY
PIE

by Valerie Hampton

Published by Country Books
an imprint of
Spiral Publishing Ltd

Country Books, 38 Pulla Hill Drive,
Storrington, West Sussex RH20 3LS

email: jonathan@spiralpublishing.com
www.spiral-books.com

ISBN 978-1-7395824-7-0

British Library Cataloguing in Publication Data.
A catalogue record for this book is available from the
British Library.

Printed and bound in England by 4edge Limited,
22 Eldon Way Industrial Estate, Hockley, Essex SS5 4AD

Contents

The Night Garden

Who knows what paths the fox will take
When in the darkness and silence
He walks, his feet no sound will make.
Only the burrowing beetle lying still
Can hear this predator passing by.
A beautiful creature, but hungry for a kill.

Along the path beneath a pitted volcanic stone
The snail will wake inside his purple shell.
Then with shining trails of silver, leave his home
But his journey to the flower beds does not go well.
A pounce that scatters the dormant ants, and he is gone,
Only the moon and the stars will see, but never tell.

The mice curled up in their dark grassy nest,
Will stir in their sleep but will not hear him pass,
So stay curled against their Mother's breast.
As the fox steps through sparkling dewy blades
The owl stares down from his leafy bough
As the sun appears behind clouds in fiery shades.

The moon has gone to join its stars in space.
Sunbeams have claimed the garden as their stage.
Night visitors must return to their hiding place.
House windows and doors are bright with light
Casting grey shadows over the lawn and beds.
But what silent creatures will be back this night?

Two Dragonflies

I saw two Dragonflies today flitting around the cherry tree
Chasing, dancing through the leaves with joy to be free.
Flashes of blue, transparent wings delicate as a new blown bubble
Twisting and turning caught by the breeze no care or trouble.
Unlike the May Fly, they have a few happy joyous weeks
Before a shadowy bird clasps them, legs trailing, in their beaks.
So dance your dance, fall on love, and feel the rays of the warming sun,
Fly with the clouds, cherish the hours, before your day is done.

The Farm

The red brick farm where we cousins stayed
Had hay barns and muddy yard, where we played.
Climbing up between bales of hay to make a den,
And talk of secret matters, important to girls of ten!
Swinging on the paddock gate as Henry and his men
Put the bull to the cow, innocence was in the air
We never knew what was going on, and we didn't care!
Down to chickens in tiny cages, their lights so bright
Never dimmed, to these poor birds there was no night.
Their white and scaley claws hanging through the mesh
To post-war shoppers these eggs were always fresh.

Most mornings happy walks, through dampened grass
Bursting puff-balls, dandelion clocks, as we pass
Mushroom picking, each carrying an ancient hessian bag,
And finding a rabbit's burrow, baby rabbits playing tag.
There worked alongside the cows and noisy herd of goats
Two young men, with bright yellow circles on their coats.
One day when in a shed, Hans had shot a rabbit dead.
We watched as he peeled off its fur, then he turned and said:
"Does your Mother say "Skin a rabbit from its vest?"
Nodding, giggling, at his strange voice, but we never guessed
That he was someone's son, a prisoner here, but blessed.

The dairy off the kitchen where Auntie sipped the cream,
Finger to her mouth, we pretended that we had never seen!
Cows when being milked had their names above their stall,
Farm cats would wait to have warm milk, no need to call!
From the cow into open mouths the milk was squirted
By Leslie the farm-hand with whom we girls flirted!
The joy of picking plums, a ride down the lane by truck
Back to the house, to read an exciting Enid Blyton book!
Dinner on a long table, the salt and pepper set had wheels!
These memories of long ago are still bright, and very clear
Childhood, so precious, must never cause a single tear.

Number 249 A Home Re-Visited

Toadflax in the mortar, blue bricks on the wall,
Yellow peeling paintwork, was that window quite so small?
The gate is off its hinges, and there's a battered rubbish bin
Memories of fireworks placed inside, and a brother's evil grin.
This the house where I was born, a shock to my siblings, three,
Who never knew that I was due, or how I came to be.

I remember the kitchen window, and walls mum painted buff
The fireplace with its two-bar fire we were never warm enough!
The dip halfway down the hall where lurked a hidden well,
"Be careful children where you tread, it may go down to HELL."
Brothers' bikes without their wheels, propped against the wall,
The cellar where we hid in case Old Hitler's bombs may fall.

The wooden doors full of holes made by brothers playing darts,
Mum's pantry full of bottled fruit, and roller skates in parts,
The meat-safe with its contents, with maggots in the meat,
Then Mum (telling lies) would shout, "It's quite alright to eat."
Alongside the safe, lay an exploded incendiary bomb,
It fell on the Gaumont cinema where Dad was number one.

The garden at 249 was a place of fun, with animals galore,
The cats always in "the family way" by the cat next-door.
Giving birth in a cardboard box while we are eating tea,
We peep under the tablecloth "There's one, no two, no THREE!"
Mum (still sipping tea) "That ginger one sadly it's born dead"
We all went on eating, it was our treat, some butter on our bread.

Mum's sisters, white-gloved, posh hats, two women six feet tall,
Would brave the bombs from Hitler and would pay 249 a call.

Auntie May would join our play, she was always very sporty,
She cartwheeled on the lawn one day, was always very naughty!
She showed off her French knickers, brothers' faces went red,
Two boys so embarrassed, they wished that they were dead!

These thoughts of chaos, all of us children free to roam.
School friends when after play, would reluctantly go home.
Memories of a cousin Joy, who dressed just like a lad,
And taught us "boogy-woogy", the neighbours thought her mad!
But I must end this reverie, of times gone by, 249 and me
"Oh thank you nurse, have I REALLY missed my cup of tea?"

I Once Loved Singing Christmas Carols

As a child the time of year when Christmas carols were being sung opened up the thoughts of twinkling lights, tinsel and the crackling of wrapping paper on the bed. Father Christmas and his sledge gliding through the starry night, bedecked with presents for all the children who had been good and kind to friends and family. Then there were visits to the church when everyone sang with a happy heart, 'Oh Little Town of Bethlehem', imagining the bright star above the darkened village, and the three Kings...'We Three Kings of Orient Are' painting them, their crowns aloft, and wearing embroidered robes of gold. Remembering all of the timeless carols, and 'singing' them silently in my head when in pain or desolation takes over, has been my way of coping. Even 'In the Bleak Midwinter', when in labour, saved my sanity. Scenes of dark trees heavy with snow, black foot marks would fill my mind, until the next pain and 'The Holly and the Ivy' followed by very un-holy and muddled tunes and verses. Chopin, Mozart, Rock-n-Roll and the Beatles would fill my mind.

However, I no longer sing carols silently in my head, they have gone, killed off by a recent stay in a hospital where dignity and care had jumped out of the windows, along with empathy and understanding. Being 'blanket' washed each early morning, just a piece of meat to be rolled from side to side. "Can you turn over?" one helper would command, then talking to her partner, "can she move...What is the matter with her?" Heads shaken. I had no identity. Neither carer knew WHAT I was suffering from, and they didn't care. I did turn to face the safety bars, my hands clinging, knuckles white, and I sang, eyes shut tightly, 'Once in Royal David's City' silently, but with fervour, then a jumbled mixture of carols, and words, while being pushed over to face my assailants. They were smiling and whispering between themselves, they were not cruel ladies. They never found out that I was paralysed below the waist.

I feel that one day I will sing carols again, not just in my head.
I hope that I will find those lovely memories of family times together
And cherish them, pushing the indignities and naked trauma of
what should have been a gentle, tender daily patient care.
That treatment has left mental scars that will live with me forever.
But scars fade, so I may be riding along with the Three Wise
Men, and singing 'God Rest Ye Merry Gentlemen' and 'Oh Little
Town...' along with my favourite carol, Christina Rossetti's words
to 'In the Bleak Midwinter' my favourite carol of all.

Insomnia

Sleep, a river of calm winding through the night
A peaceful dreamy journey until the early light...

But when the brain decides to spring alive
And become a carousel of thought in over-drive
One thought leading to another and sleep gone
Pillows like bricks, that your head can't stay on.
And that toe that is painful and bright red
Is sticking out at the bottom of the bed...

And did I put milk bottles out and lock the door
Or leave my clothes on the bathroom floor?
I never did that poly-word in the daily paper
And why has my brain decided to turn to vapour?
A thousand pictures in my mind, always revolving
Not one question is my poor brain solving...
So sleep...please come gently into my head
I will shut my eyes and get back into my bed
Take deep breaths, I may be sinking...
But NO, again I've started thinking
I may as well get up and cuddle the cat
And give the dog a friendly pat.
WHY do some people get hours of sleep?
And don't have to count those jumping sheep?
I'll eat that piece of Christmas cake,
After that cup of tea (a great mistake)
And watch bright sun arising...
I've watched before...
(That's not surprising!)
Shall I close the kitchen curtain
Will I drift off?
Well I'm...
Not...
Quite...
Certain!

A Dentist's Favourite Patient

When getting ready to sit awhile in the dentist's chair
There are all kinds of useful tips, so try to be aware
No dentist likes an onion breath, or smell a meal of curry
So brush your teeth AND tongue don't rush there's no hurry
Is your tongue a healthy red with taste buds looking rosy?
So checking up your worried face, check nostrils for any nosey!

Next and most essentially put on clean and pristine undies
No baggy grey or gardening pants, usually worn on Mondays.
For accidents can happen when lying on the tilting chair
Falls when getting down, are likely, and may need special care.
Clean those shoes before you go, brush off that doggy mess
And wear your jeans for dignity and NEVER wear a dress.

When on the slippery chair, and the drill is poised above you,
Just tell your thoughts and body, you do NOT need the loo!
Just think of better things, of shopping, handbags, and money
Block out the thoughts of wind, and a gurgling gippy tummy.
Shouting out in pain, is what we old stoics NEVER ever do.
Flinching IS allowed, and a small amount of dribbling too.

Now we cover spitting mouth-wash, after being treated.
Make sure your aim will reach the drain, never be defeated!
The nurse will stand well back in case of missed saliva
She will have seen some blood and gore, a true 'spit-survivor.'
Try not to clamp your jaw and bite the dentist's hand,
Answer his questions with gibberish, he WILL understand!

Try not to leave the surgery wearing the goggles and the bib,
Your words of thanks and praise are the usual whopping fib!
Pay the bill before you leave and take it 'on the chin'
Accept the free tube of 'dentafix,' later pop it in a bin!
Smile at the waiting patients looking terrified and scared
A quiet tear for all their worries, mutually shared.

Once home you may need a post-trauma drink.
So pour yourself wine or gin (hide the glasses in the sink!)
Don't attempt to eat that last piece of crusty bread...
Just raid the kitchen cupboards for those chocolates instead
Look brave and talk nonchalantly to friends and family
The nightmare is over for six months, you're dentally free!

Thoughts and Memories of a
Wonderful Holiday – Australia

Dear George and Dear Robyn
Here is a verse from wintery England.
(It could be much worse!)
We'd like to say THANK YOU,
To our Aussie mates
For a dream holiday,
No other equates!

Each day with you, super
Every moment exciting
So even the midges
Are excused for their biting.
The flowers, trees, the birds
So exotic and new
The wonderful mountains
Of vast misty-blue.

And of course the 'tame' lizard
Living yards from your pool
The currawongs, the mynahs...
Hanging ferns green and cool,
The lorikeets, cockatoos
King parrots so bright
Jacaranda, oleander,
And red sunsets at night.

The Opera House 'sails'
Set over the water
Sydney Bridge by the harbour
Traffic... 'lambs to the slaughter'
The River Cats smooth
On the Parramatta each day.
Admiral George in his yacht
Feet on the 'Tut' when aweigh.

That Goanna, a lizard so huge
Arriving for his dinner!
Robyn's bread so delicious
Each pudding a WINNER!
Breakfast chatter so earnest
Of 'bowels' and digestion
'Are we too fat...or too porky?'
THAT is the question.

Starry nights in the Bush
Cuddly koalas so sleepy.
Eucalyptus, frangipani...
And big spiders SO creepy!
Chicken pieces all coated
In George's herby 'brew',
The mangoes...rock melons
We ate quite a few...

This could go on forever,
There's SO much to tell
(I haven't mentioned the weather)
But I suppose I must end
All good things must finish,
These memories so happy
No years will diminish.

The Raindrop

Have you seen a raindrop sparkling between leaves of green?
Brighter than a million stars, a rainbow of colours I have seen.
Branches moving in the wind can shadow its diamond beams
But life is short for a drop of water, it can disappear like dreams.
Sometimes watching a second more, it twinkles in the setting sun
It's never seen dropping down to the earth, because its time is done.
Look hard and long at leafy trees after there has been a storm
You may see a wonder of a jewel of water, only newly born.
This magic only shines its light two heart beats from its birth,
Before it trickles off the leaf and is hidden in the earth.

Just a Social Call

"This is just a social call," the Robin said to me,
As he landed on my palm, some mealy worms for tea.
He cocked his head and puffed out his breast
His sharp beak searching for a wriggling fest.
"O' course I should be hard at work, digging in your lawn
For beetles, grubs and greenfly before the early dawn."

"But this is just a social call," the Robin said to me,
He looks at my empty palm but nothing could he see.
"Oh dear, where have they all gone, I've only eaten two...
Or was it four...or maybe three, my maths is bad that's true."
His spidery legs with needle claws, move closer to my ear.
"Shall I tell you of my darkest night of terrifying fear?"

"A lady down at number 10 sometimes throws down bread,
She has a stripey tiger cat, who would like to see me dead!
She calls it 'My Dear Boy' and 'Mummy's Little Son'
He has only got three legs, but he certainly can run!
One night he leapt at me when my beak was full of food,
He pulled out three feathers and fluff from somewhere rude!"

"But this is just a social call," the Robin shakes his feathers
"My wife is sitting on our nest, facing all types of weathers.
So I must fly, it's been so good to hear all your news,
A tasty wormy dinner too, how could any bird refuse?
But it's getting dark, the cat is out so I must go."
Off he flew into the sky, I'm sure I heard him singing
"Cheerio!"[1]

---

[1] Written for the Robin who sits on the clematis for our daily chats.

The Robin

How dark the clouds when down at heart,
The sweetest honey now tastes so tart
The rose bud withered, never to open,
The delphiniums so beautiful, lying broken.
My window isn't clear, I see the garden,
But the tears run, there is no pardon.

But a friend is sitting on a leafy bough,
His red breast proud as an old ship's prow.
His twig-like legs so straight, feet clinging,
My heart becomes joyful with his singing.
The Robin stands listening to what I say,
Of family, troubles, war death and decay.

His head cocked, his round eyes like glass,
His body lighter than a dandelion clock in grass.
No tears shed for feathers lost or main road lights,
That keep him singing through the nights.
How can I feel that the future's black,
When a friend will always come hopping back?

Remembering Medical Errors

Prick my skin. Does red blood appear?
No blood, just a salty tear.
Feel my heart, is it whole?
Is it beating with my soul?
Do my eyes see wondrous flowers?
Or a shadowy road and icy showers?
My mouth is smiling for everyone,
But my lips are dry when all are gone.
The darkness opens to let in light,
Sometimes the world is diamond bright.
These days are treasured as years ago,
But prick my skin and the tears still flow.

Lament for a Dead Possum

Oh possum, why do you lie,
On road so straight,
And there to die?

Dear friend, I am but crumpled heap,
While seeking food, a wife to keep.
A dark force hit my body hard,
My fur so soft, is now oil-tarred.
My eyes once bright, are now so dull
My vision blurred, I am just WOOL!

Oh possum dear, I see your plight,
I'll shed a tear, but GET THINGS RIGHT!
Your shiny fur of lustrous glow
Is useless now, for humans...so...
You will stay reviled by Kiwi folk
A creature fine, but a local joke!

Oh pardon ME, with my last breath,
A possum's life doesn't end with death,
We multiply so quickly that
My family large (which I begat)
Will still meander thro' gardens green
Appear on postcards...you get the scene?

So madam, do wipe your misty eye,
There are plenty more, so I do not die.
Oh possum quickly to gutter drag...
Your little body, because there is a snag.
You are in the line of speeding cars,
So hurry possum, don't gaze at stars!

But possum lay awaiting fate,
His eyes unblinking towards the pearly gate,
Then...thro' possum wool fingers
And possum wool hat, I watched in horror...
But OH DEAR....SPLAT!!!![2]

---

[2] I wrote this after we had been to New Zealand. I bought a pair of possum wool gloves and a possum wool hat. All the rage there! Possums are treated badly.

Future Medicine?

"Yes...This IS the ward, come in and sit down.
We hope you're clean and sterile,
Put on this full-length gown...
That electrical equipment is essential you know,
We monitor his heart beat,
And check the blood's flow.
He is watched very carefully for 24 hours...
He gets food thro' that tube...
Oh dear, have you brought him flowers?
How nice...but an infection may lurk in them so...
I will take them to an outside ward...
(all bacteria you know!)
Please...don't hold his hand, you might move his drips...
Thank you...Am I right...is he trying to talk?
NO...he's just moving his lips!
Oh dear...are you going?...SO soon?
You ARE very pale, I can see...
I expect you could do with a nice cup of tea?
There's a machine, dispensing lovely hot drinks,
Over there...just down the hall...
If his condition gets worse,
Shall I give you a call?[3]

---

[3] I wrote this about thirty-five years ago, when 'modern' medicine came rushing in, and touched all our lives. I can't say more.

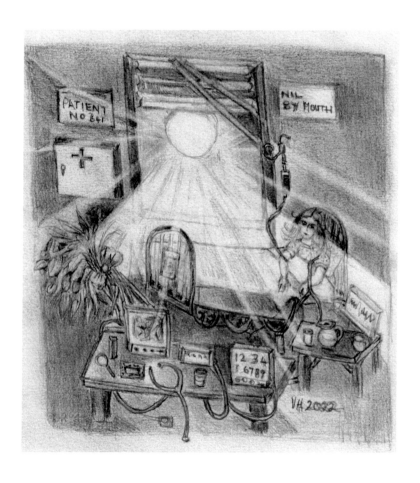

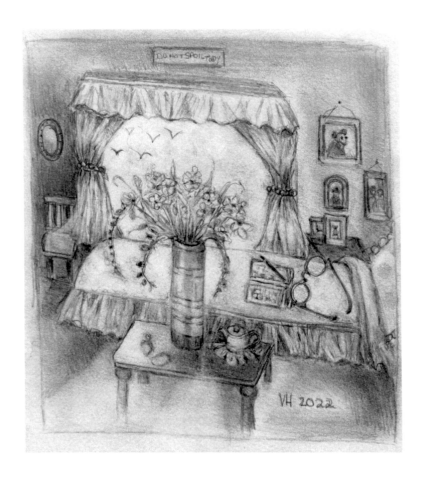

The Visitors

I enter the sunny bedroom,
Shafts of light pattern the pink bedcover.
A book of crosswords lies open,
And the scent of freesias is strong.
I can hear the voices of children,
They are playing ball beneath the window,
And there is the steady drone of a lawnmower.
Everything is so normal, so ordinary...
But Fear is here, a constant visitor,
Waiting in this sunny bedroom,
And the children go on playing,
And the neighbour continues cutting his grass.
The moon, stars, will blot out the sun,
But Hope is here, silently watching and waiting.

A declaration

No pickles, no chutney, no jelly or jam,
Oh what a terrible housewife I am!
The old worm has turned completely around,
So instead of a kitchen, on a bed I am found.
The crossword's all finished, a book almost read.
I'm not up with the lark, but lying abed.
Who cares if the apples rot under the tree,
And peas burst their pod, it won't worry ME!
The pumpkins can wither, Cinderella is dead,
And my super sharp spade, can rust in the shed.
I have picked tons of fruit and veggies galore,
Now the freezer is bursting, I can't shut the door.

But now they can wait, my Wellies can moulder,
I'm comfortable here, pillow under my shoulder.
Tonight I am heading down to an Inn
For plenty of chips, and a pre-dinner gin!
Toffee pudding will follow (bugger the weight)
Who cares at my age, too late for a date...
I'll finish with coffee, a special with choc:
Then toddle off home...trouble finding the lock...
Then on with the tele, or type a new mail.
The old worm has turned,
AND...
Become
An...old...
SNAIL!!!

A Possum's Prayer

This is a prayer from possum lowly
To HIM above who is so Holy
All creatures great and small you say,
Are watched and guarded every day,
So why am I so reviled by all?
Run down and trapped a furry ball
On roads and ditches there to die,
Are YOU watching from the sky?
And now the cruellest blow of all,
Came news that does appal!
Our little bodies are to be
Dis-membered, prepared for someone's tea?
Next, pastry, gravy, veggies too,
All will be added to the stew.

So PLEASE dear Ruler of the sky
Save me from becoming...Possum Pie!

AMEN[4]

---

[4] Written to cousin Wendy in New Zealand, who doesn't like possums!

A Bird's Prey

She would scuttle, grey-coated and twitching,
Her feet, like small creatures' feet
Her eyes, round shiny beads of jet.
My children named her 'Mouse-wife'
And would watch her, as she passed our gate
Wondering where she had tucked her grey tail?
Every morning she would hurry by, carrying two bags.
Were they full of stale cheese and bacon rind?
And we would joke, imagining what feast she carried,
But she never looked our way, just downwards
As if searching for tiny seeds, between the stones.

She doesn't pass our gate anymore.
One Sunday, during the Evensong service,
She ran into the church, and, kneeling before the Altar
Shouted in a loud, clear, human voice, imploring God to,
"Help me, please Help me Dear God".
Then the clergy, hovering and fluttering, as great birds,
Gathered up her small body,
Covering her with their white wings
And they carried her, struggling, out into the night.
And the congregation sang 'All Things Bright and Beautiful'
(Omitting verse five), and staring ahead in embarrassment.

My friends tell me that she will be well looked after,
And that 'Mental Hospitals' are much nicer these days...
But I think that the big cats have caught her,
And are playing with her shaking mind, and quivering body
As cats do, with their poor mouse victims,
And I feel ashamed.[5]

---

[5] Written about a little woman who passed our gate every day, at the same time.
Just a thought about her, not fact.

Some Hope!

I want to be a fairy,
With a wand that shines and flickers.
I want to be a fairy,
With spider's web for knickers.
I want to be a fairy,
With a headdress made from dew,
I want to be a fairy,
With a dress of petals blue.
I want to be a fairy,
And sleep in hidden bower,
I want to be a fairy,
And flit from flower to flower.
I want to be a fairy...BUT...
I fear I'm far too fat...
I'd LOVE to be a fairy...
But I'm grounded...so that's...THAT!!!!

To a Mouse

With apologies to R Burns

Wee sleekit cowering timorous beastie,
Why make my shirt a tasty feastie...
So now it barely covers my breastie...so
SCRAM...mouse...SCRAM!

Doubly incontinent on the washing,
No sense of guilt while you were noshing,
No shame whilst nibbling tatties new,
Or stuffing bird-nuts in my shoe...so
SCRAM...mouse...SCRAM!

Cower you might under noisy washer,
See this broom, it's a mousey SQUASHER.
So wee mousey, get this straight,
I'm not inclined to stand and wait...so
SCRAM...mouse...SCRAM!

So mouse, VAMOOSE...get on yer bike,
Move it buddy, take a rodent hike,
Scoot it Micky...goodbye, FAREWELL...
Adios...Ta Ta...Adieu as well...but
SCRAM...mousey....SCRAM !!!!

THE END
(But not for mousey, who scuttled out into the flowers!)[6]

---

[6] A little mouse had been for weeks filling my old gardening shoes with bird-nuts and seeds! Weeing on my washed shirt and nibbling holes in the potatoes. Of course I would never have hurt him!!

The Window

Cat on ledge, what do you see?
What green quiver of leaves holds your gaze?
Cat, do you see the silver gossamer, hanging heavy
And the working spider looping her careful pattern?
There is a daisy chain, limp and shrivelled on the grass.
Hush cat! Can you hear the echo of children's laughter,
And the sound of feet on earth and stone?

Was it only yesterday you sat, blue eyes watching,
Watching Louise, her golden hair streaming
Red dress rippling as she swung higher...then higher
To touch the apple's blossom, its petals falling?
They rest for an instant upon the star-white daisies
Around Louise's forehead,
Then they flutter, unheeded, onto the grass.

Today cat, you are sitting, fur warm against the glass.
The wizened daisies are a decaying circle now,
And the garden (so silent to my human ears),
Holds your attention with a million sounds.
I look to the sky and see billows of greyness,
But your sky is the blue of tranquillity.

Cat on ledge, I am glad you only see today,
The growing-up, the heart-break of partings,
All these I see.
Our window is the same window, but the glass in mine
Is clouded with the knowledge of mortality.
Your glass has the clearness of innocence....
Gaze on dear friend.[7]

---

[7] Written after Louise left for College.

It Can't be Changed!

I have a bright red conscience
It sits on shoulder high
And when I tell a little 'fib'
It whispers 'WHAT a LIE!'
When asked for an opinion
On a friend's new dress or hat,
I cheerfully say "beautiful"
It screams out 'WHY say THAT?'

I push it down behind me
And hope that it will shrink
When friends say 'Be a devil...
And have ANOTHER drink?'
But NO, it glows a brighter red,
How COULD I drink one more?
So I hear myself say firmly
"NO, but kind of you I'm sure."

I wish that it would disappear
For one nice carefree day,
Then I could pass that old lost dog
And look the other way!
Or walk across a busy road
When the 'green man' doesn't show
Then arrive late at the Dentist
And say my watch was slow!

I often tell it to "SHUT UP"...
GET LOST...
VAMOOSE...Please do!"
But in a voice so clear and strong
It says...
'I CAN'T...
BECAUSE...
I'M...

YOU!'

Memories

She stands, blue lupins her guardians.
Their pepper-scented pollen
Hidden for only the bee to find.
Each round leaf's centre is set
With a single diamond of dew.
And she remembers.

How often had her hands,
Child's hands, sea-shelled tipped fingers
Tilted the leaves,
Spilling the liquid diamonds,
Those fairy baths of childhood games,
Until they fell, sparkling onto the grey earth.

Her face so pale and hollow now,
Had once glowed, butter bright
Reflecting the buttercup's shiny petals,
As she burst the dandelion clock
Sending the seeds high towards the sun.
Her young breath blowing higher, into Heaven.

She stands, blue lupins her guardians.
Crystal scenes of her youth dance upon the grass,
They enfold her stooping body, warming...
She reaches out swollen fingers, feeling forgotten textures
And the lupins shed their diamonds,
Falling as tears, onto the grey earth.[8]

---

[8] This was written about Nanny LD, when she could no longer cope with her
cottage garden. She loved her blue lupins.

Reflections

Mirror, mirror on the wall,
Who is the ugliest of them all?
Where have those chestnut curls all gone?
The peach skin cheeks, and smooth white neck...
And those eyes, REALLY MINE?
They CAN'T be? Those eyes are faded, watery...
Dullness stares out, unblinking,
No bright sparkle now...what has happened?

Time has happened, and I look away quickly,
Before tears, ageless tears, show my disappointment.[9]

---

[9] A bad day, I guess!

The Moving Finger Writes

The moving finger writes; and, having writ,
Moves on: nor all your piety nor wit
Shall lure it back to cancel half a Line,
Nor all your tears wash a word of it.

The Rubaiyat. Omar Khayyam
11th Century

The deadened finger types,
And having typed, moves on.
Nor all my jollity nor wit,
Shall find the key,
To cancel half a line of it,
Nor frustrated tears
Wash out a word of it!

With humble apologies to the great Omar Khayyam.
No offence intended.

Will I suffer the fate of a thousand cuts?

21st Century

To a Friend

Gone from our house, but not from our hearts
The sun-filled window, is not so bright.
Privet shade where sleepy hours passed,
Those leafy shadows are darkness now.

No more the gentle hollow on our bedspread
Nor the softest touch of brown paw upon our faces.
No voice of morning greeting in the sunny kitchen,
Just the harsh noise of breakfast preparation.

Our friend through all our sorrow and happiness,
Yesterday you listened to sad voices, not understanding.
Farewell good companion, friend for the last twelve years.
We salute you Tai Lu, our family cat.
Our lives are darker with your passing.[10]

---

[10] *Written on the death of our beloved cat, Tai Lu. A wonderful character, a delightful boy, always remembered.*

Trains of Thought

We sat close together in that third-class carriage
On Birkenhead station, all steam and grime,
And we clasped each other, and thought of marriage...
But the train driver thought of the time...

Then you jumped off the train, with a kiss of goodbye,
Through the mist, and my tears, you looked thinner...
Then the train started off, and I thought I would die!
But the train driver thought of his dinner!![11]

---

[11] *Memories of leaving a boyfriend on Birkenhead Station. He is Anon.*

High Rise Sharps and Flats

It happened on a Christmas Eve
Not so long ago.
When Kennedy Court, in Green Street
Was blanketed with snow...
When thro' the air, o'er lofty towers
Drifts music sweet and clear.
As Arthur plays some carols
To bring back memories dear.
From Bethlehem to Winters Bleak,
Three Kings and Shepherds Flock...

Old Santa stops his reindeer,
(there's time to fill those socks!)
And Robin Redbreast stops his song,
To listen with the fox.
This night of nights is special,
To Lay and Orthodox.

Peace to every living thing,
The organ loudly thunders, and
May Arthur play his music bright,
He is one of the Seven Wonders![12]

---

[12] *This is a little tribute to Uncle Arthur Barlow, who played the organ all his life, until into his nineties.*

The mystery of the lost specs:
Or
It's an open and shut case!

*With apologies to A.A. Milne, and everyone else
who composes proper verse!
To be sung to the tune of: 'They're Changing Guard
at Buckingham Palace'*

We're hunting specs; at number thirty,
On hands and knees and getting dirty.
"I know they are only second best...
But losing them, is really a pest,"
Said Harry.

Harold is starting to shake the bushes,
We're crawling around, and getting hot flushes,
"I was picking apples off the floor,
When suddenly my vision became very poor,"
Said Harry.

Teddy is peering over the wall,
Harold joins her (because he's so tall),
"I've already searched the neighbour's flowers,
It really has taken me hours and hours,"
Said Harry.

We're hunting still at number thirty.
We are really feeling a little bit 'shirty'
"We could call in Gary, but he's out on a course,
He works much harder than Inspector Morse,"
Said Harry.

WE'VE FOUND THE SPECS
AT NUMBER THIRTY!

We're feeling much better than Burlington Bertie,
"They must have floated over the wall...
Are they intact or damaged at all?"
Asked Harry.
Now all is well at number thirty,
Teddy has washed them, they really were dirty!
"My vision is quite as good as can be...
So...thank you all, there are cakes for tea,"
Said Harry.

All my Pie, and Betty Martin
Or
Pie-eyed in Wolverhampton

Teddy and Harry came over to stay,
It was so very nice, it quite made our day.
We sat down for lunch (it was tayberry pie),
"That was good," Harry said with a lingering sigh.
So we cut some more slices...Teddy said "NO"
So just the two Harrys and I had a go!
Then away in the fridge went the pie
Still unfinished...
But Harry's pie quest was still undiminished...
So out on the table next day it was laid,
Not now with the cream, but some custard was made.
"Still yummy," said Harry, a gleam in his eye,
"There is still ONE MORE portion of tayberry pie."

But ALAS...not a space for that slice in their cases
So Teddy and Harry travelled back to their bases.
Next day, when back home, Harold hardly could wait,
So he opened the fridge and grabbed the cold plate.
No need for a dish, just a spoon and cold custard...
So the tayberry pie disappeared, quick as mustard!

(But now there's another, cooling here on the rack,
So Teddy and Harry, you will have to come back!)[13]

---

[13] This was composed after Harold's cousin Teddy and her partner, Harry, stayed for a few days. There was a glut of tayberries on the allotment. So jam and pies made, and appreciated!

Creeping and Crawling

To be sung to the tune of: 'Waltzing Matilda'

Once three jolly cockroaches crept into a garden shed
On Lord Howe Island in the middle of a sea,
And they sang as they crawled through the dust and debris:
'Who will come a creeping and crawling with me?'

CHORUS

Creeping and Crawling, Creeping and Crawling,
You'll come a Creeping and Crawling with me,
And they sang as they danced and ate a pile of compost,
We will come a Creeping and Crawling you'll see!

Up came the gardener, saw all their legs awaving,
"Gotcha you roaches you'll never crawl on ME".
He threw them into a rubbish bin, laughing as he shut the door,
"There'll be no more creeping as I'm going for my tea".

CHORUS

Up strode the gardener's wife, red-faced and angry,
Followed by their children, one, two, three.
And they sang as they danced out into the garden.
Then they sang as they threw them under a tree.

CHORUS

Up flew the currawongs crowing with excitement,
As they gobbled up their dinner, one, two, three!
And on a moonlit night from inside the gardener's shed
BABY roaches are heard as they chant in revelry.

CHORUS

'You'll not get rid of us, we are as happy as can be'
And they sang as they gobbled up EVERYTHING!
And their songs echoed around the frosty garden,
'We'll be a Creeping and Crawling JUST YOU SEE!'

CHORUS[14]

---

[14] A skit on the song 'Waltzing Matilda'. Cockroaches are left to die in George's shed on Lord Howe Island – so I let them out into the garden, probably stamped on by George!

No Place Like Home

Sam sat on his wooden perch
Alone in his cage, and feeling sad.
He looked in his mirror and rang his bell,
Ate his seeds, and felt like hell.

He looked at the door and the open space,
Fluffed up his feathers and spread his wings.
Then out he flew into some windy weather,
Not caring when his tail lost a feather!

The city beckoned with its twinkling lights,
Sam had heard about the gambling dens,
Casinos, pubs and darkened places,
Fast cars and unsmiling faces.

So Sam drove a Porsche, drank some beer,
Played roulette, and ate too many burgers,
Strutted his stuff but didn't feel fine,
Was it bird flu or too much wine?

So with droopy wings and bleary eyes,
He left the music and glittering lights.
The darkening sky, heavy with rain,
Sam longed for his cage and swing again.

So Sam set off home, wet and weary,
His wings felt heavy, and his heart was racing.
Back in his cage so warm and cosy,
He lay on the sawdust feeling dozy.

And that's where the family found him.
"Fetch the vet," called a frightened dad.
"He looks starved, look at his open beak."
The vet arrived and said, "Sam's future's bleak".

"I know," said Mum. "I think he's lonely,
I'll get him a wife, to keep him company."
So Jane arrived all green, young and sleek,
They sit together on the swing, cheek to cheek.

Sam no longer longs for the fast cars and wine.
The cage door is open wide, no urge to fly outside.
No yearning for the 'flesh pots' of the city.
Who needs it, when you have a wife so very pretty?

Leaning

I would love a dog to lean against,
And the dog to lean on me.
To feel the warm and silky head
Heavy on my knee.
Would he know what sadness is
Or shed tears of sorrow?
And would his paw upon my hand
Stop the fears of our tomorrow?

THE END

Acknowledgments

I am so grateful to all my friends and family over the years who have provided me with so many fond memories and helped me through difficult times. Particular thanks to my patient husband Harold and children Robin and Louise and, in turn, their own families who have helped me have the confidence and tools to enable me to finally get my words onto paper.